Vilnius, Travel Guide

Discovering Vilnius: A Comprehensive Guide to Lithuania's Capital City

WANDER WORDS

OVERVIEW

"Discovering Vilnius: A Comprehensive Guide to Lithuania's Capital City" is your ultimate companion to exploring the vibrant and historic city of Vilnius, Lithuania. This guidebook offers a detailed and engaging overview of Vilnius, including its rich history and culture, top attractions, outdoor activities, food and drink scene, accommodation options, and practical information for travelers.

Discover Vilnius' captivating past and present through its UNESCO World Heritage Site status, architecture, landmarks, museums, and thriving arts scene in this insightful guidebook.

In addition, the book offers recommendations for outdoor activities, including hiking, biking, river cruises, and winter sports. The food and drink section covers Lithuanian cuisine, local specialties, and the best restaurants and bars in Vilnius.

The practical information section includes tips on money and tipping, health and safety, language and communication, and local customs and etiquette. The guidebook also includes useful phrases and vocabulary to help readers navigate Vilnius with ease.

For those looking to venture beyond Vilnius, the book features day trip recommendations to nearby destinations, including Trakai, Kernavė, Anykščiai, and Druskininkai.

Whether you're a first-time visitor or a seasoned traveler to Vilnius, this guide provides all the information and inspiration you need to make the most of your trip.

CONTENTS

INTRODUCTION

Welcome to Vilnius, the charming capital of Lithuania! Nestled in the heart of the Baltics, Vilnius is a city that effortlessly blends old-world charm with modern sophistication. As you stroll through its winding cobblestone streets, you'll discover a treasure trove of historical and cultural attractions, stunning architecture, and a vibrant food and drink scene. Whether you're a history buff, an art lover, or simply seeking a unique adventure, Vilnius has something to offer everyone. In this travel guide, we'll take you on a journey through Vilnius and provide you with all the information you need to make the most of your trip. Let's explore!

About Vilnius

Vilnius is the capital and largest city of Lithuania, a small country located in northeastern Europe. With a population of just over half a million people, Vilnius is a relatively small capital city, but it is known for its rich history, stunning architecture, and vibrant culture. The city is situated in the southeastern part of the country and is surrounded by rolling hills and forests, making it a picturesque destination for nature lovers.

Vilnius has a long and fascinating history that dates back to the 14th century, when it was first mentioned in historical records. Over the centuries, the city has been ruled by various empires and countries, including Poland, Russia, and Germany, and each of these periods has left its mark on the city's culture and architecture.

Today, Vilnius is a thriving cultural and economic hub, with a diverse population that includes Lithuanians, Russians, Poles, and other ethnic groups. The city is home to numerous museums, galleries, and theaters, as well as a bustling food and drink scene that showcases the best of Lithuanian cuisine.

Whether you're interested in history, culture, nature, or simply want to experience a new destination, Vilnius is a city that should not be missed. In the following chapters, we'll take a closer look at some of the city's top attractions, outdoor activities, food and drink scene, and much more.

When to visit

Vilnius is a destination that can be visited year-round, but the best time to visit depends on your personal preferences and interests.

Summer (June-August) is the high season for tourism in Vilnius, as the weather is warm and sunny, and there are numerous outdoor festivals and events. However, this also means that the city can be quite crowded, and accommodation prices tend to be higher than during the rest of the year.

If you prefer cooler temperatures and fewer crowds, consider visiting Vilnius in the spring (April-May) or autumn (September-November). During these seasons, the weather is mild and pleasant, and you can still enjoy many outdoor activities and cultural events. Additionally, hotel prices tend to be lower during these months, making it a great time to visit on a budget.

Winter (December-March) is a unique and magical time to visit Vilnius, especially if you're a fan of winter sports and holiday festivities. The city transforms into a winter wonderland, with Christmas markets, ice skating rinks, and festive decorations throughout the city. Additionally, the nearby ski resorts of Snow Arena and Liepkalnis are popular destinations for skiing, snowboarding, and other winter sports.

The best time to visit Vilnius depends on your personal preferences and interests. Each season has its own unique charms and attractions, so consider what you want to see and do before deciding when to book your trip.

Getting there

Getting to Vilnius is easy, as the city is well-connected to other major cities in Europe and beyond.

By Air:

Vilnius International Airport (VNO) is the main airport serving the city and is located just 7 km south of the city center. The airport serves numerous international airlines, including budget carriers such as Ryanair and Wizz Air, making it an affordable option for budget-conscious travelers. From the airport, you can reach the city center by bus, train, or taxi.

By Train:

Vilnius is also accessible by train, with regular connections to other major cities in Lithuania and neighboring countries such as Latvia, Estonia, and Belarus. The main train station in Vilnius is located in the city center and is well-connected to the rest of the city by public transport.

By Bus:

Vilnius has a well-developed bus network, with regular connections to other cities in Lithuania and neighboring countries. The main bus station is located just outside the city center and is easily accessible by public transport.

By Car:

If you prefer to drive, Vilnius is easily accessible by car, with good roads connecting it to other major cities in Lithuania and neighboring countries. However, be aware that traffic can be heavy during peak hours, and parking in the city center can be difficult and expensive.

Getting to Vilnius is easy, with numerous transportation options available to suit different budgets and preferences. Whether you choose to fly, take the train or bus, or drive, you'll find that Vilnius is easily accessible from most major cities in Europe and beyond.

Getting around

Getting around Vilnius is easy and convenient, thanks to the city's well-developed public transport system.

Public Transport:

The most common mode of transport in Vilnius is the bus, which serves almost every part of the city. There are also trolleybuses and trams, although their routes are more limited. You can purchase tickets from kiosks or directly from the driver, and fares are relatively affordable. If you plan on using public transport frequently during your stay, consider purchasing a Vilnius City Card, which includes unlimited public transport use and discounts on attractions and restaurants.

Taxi:

Taxis are widely available in Vilnius, although they can be expensive compared to public transport. Make sure to only use licensed taxi companies, and be aware that taxi drivers may not speak English. You can also use ride-hailing services such as Uber or Bolt, which are typically cheaper than traditional taxis.

Bicycle:

Cycling is a popular mode of transport in Vilnius, and the city has an extensive network of bike lanes and bike rental services. Renting a bike is an affordable and eco-friendly way to explore the city, and there are many scenic bike routes that take you through parks and along the river.

Walking:

Finally, walking is a great way to explore the historic Old Town of Vilnius, which is a pedestrian-only area. Walking allows you to fully appreciate the city's stunning architecture and charming cobblestone streets, and there are many guided walking tours available that provide insights into the city's history and culture.

Getting around Vilnius is easy and convenient, with numerous transportation options available to suit different preferences and budgets. Whether you choose to take the bus, taxi, bike, or walk, you'll find that getting around the city is a breeze.

HISTORY AND CULTURE

Vilnius is a city rich in history and culture, with a fascinating blend of architectural styles and cultural traditions that reflect its complex past. From its medieval Old Town to its modern art galleries and museums, Vilnius offers a wealth of cultural experiences for visitors to explore. In this section, we'll delve into the city's rich history and culture, exploring its diverse neighborhoods, iconic landmarks, and unique cultural traditions that make it one of the most fascinating destinations in Europe.

The history of Vilnius

Vilnius has a rich and complex history that spans over 1,000 years, shaped by the influence of different cultures and civilizations that have left their mark on the city. The earliest records of Vilnius date back to the 10th century when it was a small fortress on the banks of the Neris River. Over the centuries, Vilnius grew in size and importance, becoming the capital of the Grand Duchy of Lithuania in the 14th century.

One of the most important periods in Vilnius' history was the Renaissance, when the city experienced a cultural and artistic reawakening. Many of the city's most iconic landmarks, including the Vilnius University and the Church of St. Anne, were built during this time, and the city became a center of learning and culture.

In the 20th century, Vilnius underwent significant changes as it was occupied by different powers. During World War II, the city was occupied by Nazi Germany, and many of its Jewish inhabitants were killed in the Holocaust. After the war, Vilnius became part of the Soviet Union, and the city underwent significant urbanization and modernization.

Since Lithuania regained its independence in 1990, Vilnius has undergone a transformation, with many of its historic buildings restored and its cultural traditions revived. Today, Vilnius is a vibrant and cosmopolitan city, with a rich history and culture that make it one of the most fascinating destinations in Europe.

Vilnius' history is a complex tapestry of different cultures and civilizations that have left their mark on the city. From its medieval origins to its Renaissance golden age and its modern-day revival, Vilnius is a city that has undergone significant changes over the centuries, yet has managed to retain its unique cultural identity.

Architecture and landmarks

Vilnius is a city with a rich architectural heritage, with buildings and landmarks that reflect its complex history and cultural influences. The city's Old Town, which is a UNESCO World Heritage Site, is a maze of winding streets and alleyways that are home to some of the most stunning examples of Gothic, Renaissance, Baroque, and neoclassical architecture in Europe.

One of the most iconic landmarks in Vilnius is the Vilnius Cathedral, which dates back to the 14th century and has been rebuilt and renovated several times throughout history. Another notable landmark is the Gediminas Castle Tower, which is perched on a hill overlooking the city and offers panoramic views of the Old Town.

The Church of St. Anne is another must-see landmark in Vilnius. This stunning Gothic masterpiece was built in the 15th century and is known for its intricate brickwork and delicate arches. Other notable religious buildings in Vilnius include the Orthodox Church of the Holy Spirit and the Baroque-style Church of St. Peter and St. Paul.

Vilnius is a city with a wealth of architectural and cultural landmarks that reflect its complex history and cultural influences. From the Gothic splendor of the

Church of St. Anne to the panoramic views from the Gediminas Castle Tower, Vilnius is a city that is sure to leave a lasting impression on visitors.

Museums and galleries

Vilnius is a city with a rich cultural heritage, and there are many museums and galleries throughout the city that showcase its history and art. Whether you're interested in ancient history, modern art, or anything in between, there's something for everyone in Vilnius.

One of the most popular museums in Vilnius is the National Museum of Lithuania. This museum houses a vast collection of artifacts that tell the story of Lithuania's history, from prehistoric times to the present day. The museum is housed in a stunning neoclassical building in the heart of the Old Town, making it a must-visit destination for anyone interested in history.

For art lovers, the National Art Gallery is a must-see destination in Vilnius. This gallery houses a collection of Lithuanian art from the 16th century to the present day, including paintings, sculptures, and other works of art. The gallery also hosts temporary exhibitions throughout the year, so there's always something new to see.

Another popular museum in Vilnius is the Museum of Genocide Victims. Housed in the former KGB headquarters, this museum offers a sobering glimpse into the city's dark past under Soviet rule. Visitors can explore the prison cells, torture rooms, and other areas of the building where political prisoners were held and interrogated.

For something a bit different, the Museum of Illusions is a fun and interactive museum that offers a unique experience for visitors of all ages. Visitors can explore a variety of optical illusions and interactive exhibits that will challenge their perception and leave them amazed.

Vilnius is a city with a rich cultural heritage, and there are many museums and galleries throughout the city that showcase its history and art. Whether you're interested in ancient history, modern art, or something in between, Vilnius has something to offer every visitor.

The arts scene

Vilnius is a city that has long been known for its vibrant arts scene, with a rich cultural heritage that spans centuries. Today, the city is home to a thriving community of artists, writers, and musicians, who draw inspiration from the city's history and cultural influences.

One of the best places to experience the arts scene in Vilnius is the Arts Printing House, a cultural center that showcases contemporary Lithuanian theater, dance, and music. This venue hosts a variety of events throughout the year, including concerts, plays, and dance performances, making it a must-visit destination for anyone interested in the performing arts.

For those interested in the visual arts, the Vilnius Picture Gallery is a must-see destination. This gallery houses a collection of Lithuanian and international art from the 16th century to the present day, including paintings, sculptures, and other works of art. The gallery also hosts temporary exhibitions throughout the year, so there's always something new to see.

The city is also home to a thriving street art scene, with murals and graffiti adorning buildings throughout the city. The Užupis neighborhood, known for its bohemian vibe and artistic community, is a great place to explore the city's street art scene.

In addition to the galleries and performance venues, Vilnius is also home to several literary events and festivals throughout the year. The Vilnius Book Fair is one of the largest and most prestigious literary events in the region, attracting authors, publishers, and book lovers from around the world.

Vilnius is a city with a thriving arts scene that draws inspiration from its rich cultural heritage. Whether you're interested in theater, dance, music, or the visual arts, there's something for everyone in Vilnius. With its vibrant street art scene and numerous festivals and events, Vilnius is a city that is sure to inspire and delight visitors.

TOP ATTRACTIONS

Vilnius is a city with a rich history and cultural heritage, and there are many attractions throughout the city that showcase its beauty and charm. From the medieval Old Town to the modern museums and galleries, Vilnius has something for every type of traveler. In this section, we'll take a look at some of the top attractions in Vilnius that should not be missed during your visit.

Vilnius Old Town(54°41'13.9"N 25°16'46.9"E)

Vilnius Old Town is a UNESCO World Heritage Site and one of the most popular destinations in Vilnius. With its winding cobblestone streets, colorful buildings, and charming courtyards, it's easy to see why. The Old Town is home to many of Vilnius' top attractions, including historic churches, palaces, and museums.

One of the most notable landmarks in the Old Town is the Vilnius Cathedral, which dates back to the 13th century. The cathedral has been rebuilt several times over the centuries, with the current neoclassical façade dating back to the 18th century. Visitors can explore the interior of the cathedral, which houses a number of important religious relics and works of art.

Another must-see attraction in the Old Town is the Gediminas Tower, which is located on a hill overlooking the city. The tower was originally built in the 14th century as part of the city's defensive fortifications, and today it serves as a museum and observation deck. Visitors can climb to the top of the tower for stunning views of the city and the surrounding countryside.

The Old Town is also home to many beautiful churches, including St. Anne's Church, which is considered to be one of the finest examples of Gothic architecture in Lithuania. The Church of St. Peter and St. Paul is another popular attraction, known for its ornate Baroque interior and impressive ceiling frescoes.

There are also many restaurants, cafes, and bars throughout the Old Town that offer traditional Lithuanian dishes and local craft beers.

Vilnius Old Town is a must-visit destination for

anyone traveling to Vilnius. With its charming architecture, historic landmarks, and vibrant culture, it's easy to spend hours exploring the winding streets and hidden courtyards of this UNESCO World Heritage Site.

Gediminas Castle Tower(54°41'13.7"N 25°17'27.6"E)

Perched on a hill overlooking Vilnius, the Gediminas Castle Tower is one of the city's most recognizable landmarks. The tower dates back to the 14th century and was once part of a larger defensive fortress that protected the city from invaders. Today, the tower serves as a museum and observation deck, offering stunning views of Vilnius and the surrounding countryside.

To reach the top of the tower, visitors must climb a steep staircase that winds through the interior. Along the way, there are several exhibitions that showcase the history of the tower and the city of Vilnius. The top of the tower is an open-air observation deck that provides panoramic views of the city and the nearby hills.

The views from the top of the tower are truly breathtaking, and visitors can see many of Vilnius' top attractions, including the Cathedral of St. Stanislaus and St. Ladislaus, the Palace of the Grand Dukes of Lithuania, and the Vilnius Old Town. The tower is also a great spot to watch the sunset over the city.

In addition to the tower itself, the Gediminas Castle complex includes several other historic buildings and attractions. These include the Royal Palace of Lithuania, which was the residence of the Grand Duke of Lithuania in the 15th century, and the Lithuanian National Museum, which houses exhibits on Lithuanian history and culture.

Visiting the Gediminas Castle Tower is a must-do activity for anyone traveling to Vilnius. The views from the top are stunning, and the history of the tower and the castle complex provide a fascinating glimpse into Lithuania's rich cultural heritage.

St. Anne's Church(54°40'60.0"N 25°17'35.0"E)

St. Anne's Church is a stunning example of Gothic architecture located in the heart of Vilnius' Old Town. Built in the 15th century, the church is widely regarded as one of the most beautiful buildings in Lithuania, and it's easy to see why.

The church's façade features intricate stone carvings and decorative elements that are truly awe-inspiring. The interior of the church is no less impressive, with soaring vaulted ceilings and stained-glass windows that cast a colorful glow throughout the space.

Legend has it that Napoleon Bonaparte was so

taken with St. Anne's Church that he wanted to take it back to France with him. While this story may be apocryphal, it speaks to the church's enduring appeal and the awe it inspires in visitors.

One of the unique features of St. Anne's Church is its acoustics. The church's architecture is such that even the quietest whisper can be heard throughout the entire space. This feature has made St. Anne's Church a popular venue for classical music concerts and other performances.

Visitors to St. Anne's Church can take a guided tour of the interior or attend a mass, which is held daily. The church is also surrounded by a number of cafes and restaurants, making it a great spot to relax and enjoy the atmosphere of Vilnius' Old Town.

St. Anne's Church is a must-see attraction for anyone visiting Vilnius. Its stunning Gothic architecture and rich history make it a true gem of Lithuania's cultural heritage.

Vilnius Cathedral(54°41'09.6"N 25°17'15.9"E)

Vilnius Cathedral, also known as the Cathedral of St. Stanislaus and St. Ladislaus, is one of the most important religious and cultural landmarks in Vilnius. The cathedral's grand neoclassical façade is an iconic symbol of the city, and its interior is equally impressive.

The cathedral has a long and storied history that dates back to the 14th century. Over the years, it has been destroyed and rebuilt several times, with each iteration adding new elements to its architecture and design. Today, the cathedral is an impressive blend of Gothic, Baroque, and neoclassical styles.

Visitors to the cathedral can explore its interior, which is adorned with stunning frescoes, intricate carvings, and beautiful stained-glass windows. The cathedral also houses several important works of art, including a painting of the Madonna and Child by the famous Lithuanian artist Mikalojus Konstantinas Čiurlionis.

One of the most notable features of Vilnius Cathedral is its crypt, which contains the tombs of many of Lithuania's most important historical figures, including Grand Duke Gediminas, the founder of Vilnius. The crypt also houses a museum that explores the history of the cathedral and its role in Lithuanian culture.

Vilnius Cathedral is also an important political landmark. It has served as the site of many important events in Lithuania's history, including the coronation of Lithuania's kings and the signing of the country's first constitution.

Visiting Vilnius Cathedral is a must-do activity for anyone traveling to Vilnius. Its grand architecture, rich history, and cultural significance make it a true gem of Lithuania's cultural heritage.

Užupis District(54°40'48.0"N 25°17'39.1"E)

Užupis is one of the most unique and creative districts of Vilnius. This bohemian neighborhood is known for its quirky street art, colorful buildings, and laid-back vibe. In fact, it has even declared itself an independent republic, complete with its own constitution, president, and flag!

The district's history is as interesting as its present. It was once a rundown area of Vilnius, inhabited by artists, musicians, and other creatives who were drawn to its cheap rent and bohemian atmosphere. Over time, these residents transformed the neighborhood into a vibrant cultural hub, filled with art galleries, cafes, and studios.

Today, Užupis is a must-visit destination for anyone interested in art, culture, and offbeat travel experiences. Visitors can spend hours exploring the district's winding streets, admiring the colorful street art, and browsing the unique shops and boutiques.

One of the most iconic features of Užupis is its central square, which is home to the "Angel of Užupis" statue. This bronze sculpture, which stands at the heart of the district, symbolizes the spirit of Užupis and its commitment to artistic freedom and creativity.

Užupis is also home to several galleries and art spaces, including the Užupis Art Incubator, which showcases the work of up-and-coming artists from around the world. Visitors can also explore the Užupis Constitution, which is displayed in several languages on a wall in the district and outlines the principles of the independent republic.

Whether you're interested in art, history, or just want to experience the offbeat charm of Vilnius, a visit to Užupis is a must-do activity. This unique neighborhood is a true gem of Lithuania's cultural landscape.

Trakai Castle(54°39'09.0"N 24°56'00.8"E)

Located just 28 kilometers west of Vilnius, Trakai Castle is a must-visit destination for history buffs and architecture enthusiasts. This stunning fortress, built in the 14th century, sits on a small island in the middle of Lake Galvė and is one of the most iconic landmarks in Lithuania.

The castle was originally constructed as a defensive fortress for the Grand Duchy of Lithuania, and over the years it has served as a royal residence, a prison, and even a military barracks. Today, it is a popular tourist attraction and a UNESCO World Heritage Site.

Visitors to Trakai Castle can explore the castle's

many rooms and courtyards, which are filled with fascinating historical artifacts and exhibits. Highlights include the castle's impressive Great Hall, which is adorned with intricate carvings and frescoes, and the impressive towers, which offer stunning views of the surrounding countryside.

In addition to exploring the castle itself, visitors can also take a boat tour of Lake Galvė, or rent a paddleboat to explore the lake on their own. The lake is surrounded by beautiful forests and rolling hills, making it a popular spot for hiking, biking, and other outdoor activities.

Trakai Castle is a must-visit destination for anyone interested in history, architecture, or just looking for a beautiful day trip from Vilnius. With its stunning location, fascinating history, and beautiful surroundings, it's a true gem of Lithuania's cultural heritage.

Museum of Occupations and Freedom Fights(54°41'17.2"N 25°16'14.0"E)

The KGB Museum, also known as the Genocido Auku Muziejus, is a museum located in the heart of Vilnius, Lithuania. The museum was established in 1992 to document the Soviet occupation of Lithuania, and to commemorate the victims of genocide during this time.

The museum is housed in the former KGB headquarters, where political prisoners were interrogated and tortured during the Soviet occupation. Visitors to the museum can explore the prison cells, torture rooms, and execution chamber, as well as view exhibits that tell the stories of the victims of the KGB's terror.

The museum offers a stark reminder of Lithuania's dark past, and serves as a testament to the resilience of the Lithuanian people. It is a must-visit for anyone interested in the history of Lithuania, the Soviet occupation, and the struggle for freedom and independence. The KGB Museum is one of the most popular attractions in Vilnius and is sure to leave a lasting impression on all who visit.

OUTDOOR ACTIVITIES

The city also offers plenty of opportunities to get outside and explore the great outdoors. Whether you're looking to hike, bike, or simply take a leisurely stroll, Vilnius and its surrounding areas have something for everyone. From tranquil parks to rugged hiking trails, the city's outdoor offerings are sure to delight visitors of all ages and interests.

Parks and gardens

Vilnius is a city that prides itself on its green spaces, with numerous parks and gardens located throughout the city. Whether you're looking for a quiet spot to relax and enjoy nature or a place to take the kids for a picnic, there are plenty of options to choose from.

One of the most popular parks in Vilnius is Vingis

Park, located just a few kilometers west of the city center. This sprawling green space covers over 160 hectares and is home to numerous walking and cycling paths, as well as playgrounds, sports fields, and a small lake. In the summer months, the park hosts a variety of outdoor concerts and festivals, making it a favorite destination for locals and tourists alike.

Another must-visit park in Vilnius is Bernardinai Gardens, located in the heart of the Old Town. This beautiful park is home to numerous walking paths, ornamental fountains, and lush gardens, making it the perfect spot to take a break from sightseeing and enjoy a peaceful afternoon.

For those looking to escape the hustle and bustle of the city, Grutas Park is a unique destination located about an hour's drive southwest of Vilnius. This open-air museum and park is home to numerous Soviet-era sculptures and monuments, making it a fascinating place to explore for anyone interested in history or political art.

Vilnius is a city that values its green spaces, and visitors are sure to find a park or garden that suits their interests and needs. Whether you're looking to relax, exercise, or simply take in the natural beauty of the city, Vilnius has something for everyone.

Hiking and biking trails

Vilnius and its surrounding areas are home to some truly stunning natural landscapes, making it a popular destination for outdoor enthusiasts. Whether you're an experienced hiker or biker, or simply looking for a scenic walk, there are plenty of trails to choose from.

One popular destination for hikers and bikers alike is the Verkiai Regional Park, located just a few kilometers north of Vilnius. This beautiful park covers over 1,000 hectares of forests, lakes, and rivers, and is home to a variety of hiking and biking trails suitable for all skill levels. Some of the most popular routes in the park include the Verkiai Palace Trail, which leads visitors past a historic palace and stunning views of the Neris River, and the Šilėnai Forest Trail, which winds through dense forests and open fields.

Another popular hiking destination is the Vilnius TV Tower, located just a few kilometers south of the city center. This towering structure offers stunning views of the surrounding countryside and is accessible via a steep but rewarding hike up a nearby hill.

For cyclists, the Green Lakes Route is a must-visit destination. This 17-kilometer trail winds through forests and along the shores of several lakes, offering stunning views of the surrounding countryside. The trail is suitable for riders of all skill levels and is a popular destination for both locals and tourists.

Vilnius and its surrounding areas offer plenty of opportunities to get outside and explore the great outdoors. With hiking and biking trails suitable for all skill levels, visitors are sure to find a route that suits their interests and abilities.

River cruises

One of the best ways to experience the beauty of Vilnius is by taking a river cruise along the Neris River. The river flows through the heart of the city, offering stunning views of its historic architecture and scenic landscapes. There are several tour operators in Vilnius that offer river cruises of varying lengths and prices, ranging from one-hour sightseeing tours to multi-day excursions.

A popular option for tourists is the Vilnius Panorama Tour, which takes visitors on a one-hour scenic cruise along the Neris River. The tour departs from the Cathedral Square and offers stunning views of Vilnius Old Town, the Gediminas Castle Tower, and other major landmarks. Along the way, visitors can learn about the city's history and culture from an onboard guide.

For those who want to spend more time on the water, there are also longer river cruises available that explore more of the Neris River and its surrounding areas. These tours may include stops at historic sites, such as Trakai Island Castle, or visits to local villages and towns along the river.

There are also dinner and cocktail cruises available,

where visitors can enjoy a meal or drink while taking in the stunning views of Vilnius by night. These cruises are a romantic and memorable way to experience the city's beauty and charm.

A river cruise is a unique and enjoyable way to experience Vilnius and its surrounding areas. Whether you're interested in sightseeing, dining, or exploring the city's history and culture, there is a river cruise that will suit your interests and budget.

Winter sports

While Vilnius may not be known for its winter sports scene, there are still plenty of opportunities for outdoor enthusiasts to enjoy the snowy season. One popular winter activity in Vilnius is ice skating, with several rinks located throughout the city. The most popular rink is located in the city center, near the Vilnius Cathedral, and is open from November to March.

For those who enjoy skiing or snowboarding, there are several ski resorts within a few hours' drive of Vilnius. The most popular resort is Snow Arena in Druskininkai, which features an indoor ski slope, as well as outdoor runs and other winter activities. Snow Arena is located approximately 130 kilometers (80 miles) south of Vilnius and is accessible by car or public transportation.

Another popular winter activity in Vilnius is cross-country skiing. There are several parks and nature reserves located within the city and its surrounding areas that offer groomed trails for cross-country skiing. One popular location for cross-country skiing is the Belmontas Park, located approximately 10 kilometers (6 miles) from the city center. The park features several trails that wind through its scenic forests and along the Vilnia River.

While Vilnius may not have a well-developed winter sports scene, there are still plenty of opportunities to enjoy outdoor activities during the winter months. From ice skating to skiing to cross-country skiing, there is something for everyone to enjoy in Vilnius in the wintertime.

FOOD AND DRINK

Lithuanian cuisine is a delicious blend of hearty, rustic flavors and traditional recipes that have been passed down for generations. Vilnius, as the capital city, offers visitors a diverse range of dining options, from cozy cafes and casual pubs to upscale restaurants that showcase the best of Lithuanian cuisine.

In addition to traditional Lithuanian dishes, Vilnius is also home to a thriving international food scene, with restaurants and cafes featuring cuisine from all over the world. From Asian-inspired street food to classic Italian pasta dishes, there is something for everyone to enjoy in Vilnius.

Of course, no visit to Vilnius would be complete without trying some of the city's signature dishes and drinks, such as cepelinai (potato dumplings stuffed with meat), šaltibarščiai (cold beet soup), and

Lithuanian beer, which is known for its rich flavor and high quality.

Whether you're looking for a quick snack or a leisurely meal, Vilnius has plenty of options to satisfy your appetite. So come hungry and get ready to discover the delicious flavors of Vilnius!

Lithuanian cuisine

Lithuanian cuisine is a reflection of the country's agricultural roots, with a focus on hearty, filling dishes that make use of local ingredients. Many Lithuanian dishes are made with potatoes, which are a staple in the country's cuisine.

One of the most famous Lithuanian dishes is cepelinai, which are large potato dumplings stuffed with meat, cheese, or mushrooms. Another popular dish is kugelis, a potato pudding that is typically served with bacon or sour cream.

Meat dishes are also common in Lithuanian cuisine, with pork being the most popular meat. Cepelinai can also be made with pork filling, and other meat dishes include koldūnai (meat-filled dumplings) and šaltiena (a jellied meat dish).

Lithuanian cuisine also features a variety of soups, including šaltibarščiai, a cold beet soup that is perfect for summer days. Other soups include bulvės (potato soup), grybų sriuba (mushroom soup), and žirnių sriuba (pea soup).

Lithuanians also have a sweet tooth, with desserts like šakotis (a spiral cake) and kūčiukai (small sweet bread rolls) being popular during holidays and celebrations.

In terms of drinks, Lithuanian beer is world-renowned for its high quality and rich flavor. The country also produces its own spirits, including krupnikas (a honey liqueur) and starka (a traditional Lithuanian vodka).

Lithuanian cuisine is a delicious reflection of the country's history and culture, and visitors to Vilnius should definitely try some of the local specialties during their stay.

Local specialties

Vilnius, like the rest of Lithuania, has a rich culinary tradition with many local specialties worth trying. Here are some dishes to look out for during your visit:

Cepelinai - Also known as "zeppelins" due to their shape, these are large potato dumplings filled with meat, cheese, or mushrooms and typically served with sour cream or bacon.

Kugelis - A potato pudding made with grated potatoes, eggs, milk, and bacon or pork fat. Often served with sour cream or apple sauce.

Šaltibarščiai - A cold soup made with beets, kefir or buttermilk, cucumbers, and dill. Often served with boiled potatoes and hard-boiled eggs.

Koldūnai - Dumplings filled with meat or mushrooms and served with sour cream or butter. They can be boiled, fried, or baked.

Balandėliai - Cabbage rolls stuffed with ground meat, rice, and vegetables, often served with tomato sauce.

Skilandis - A smoked meat sausage made from pork and flavored with garlic and other spices.

Šakotis - A spiral-shaped cake made by pouring batter onto a rotating spit over an open flame.

There are also many sweet treats worth trying like Christmas-favorite kūčiukai and celebratory layered honey cake, paired perfectly with locally brewed Lithuanian beer or traditional spirits like krupnikas and starka.

Best restaurants and cafes

Vilnius has a vibrant food scene with plenty of options to suit every taste and budget. Here are some of the best restaurants and cafes in the city:

Sweet Root - A fine-dining restaurant that serves

modern Lithuanian cuisine made with locally sourced ingredients.

Džiaugsmas - A cozy restaurant that offers a mix of traditional Lithuanian and modern European cuisine, with an emphasis on seasonal and locally sourced ingredients.

Bernelių užeiga - A chain of Lithuanian restaurants that serve hearty traditional dishes like cepelinai, kugelis, and koldūnai.

Kitchen - A popular restaurant that offers a variety of international dishes, with an emphasis on Asian cuisine.

Lokys - A historic restaurant that specializes in game dishes like venison, wild boar, and elk.

Coffee1 - A popular cafe chain that serves a variety of coffee drinks, sandwiches, salads, and pastries.

Holy Donut - A trendy cafe that offers a variety of homemade donuts and coffee drinks.

These are just a few of the many great dining options in Vilnius. Be sure to also explore the city's many markets and food stalls, where you can sample local specialties and fresh produce.

Bars and nightlife

Vilnius has a thriving nightlife scene, with plenty of bars and clubs to suit every taste. Here are some of the best places to enjoy a night out in the city:

Alchemikas - A cozy cocktail bar that offers a variety of unique and creative drinks, with an emphasis on locally sourced ingredients.

Pabo Latino - A lively Latin dance club that plays salsa, bachata, and reggaeton music.

Dirty Duck - A popular sports bar that offers a variety of beers on tap and a relaxed atmosphere.

Bukowski Bar - A hipster-friendly bar that serves a variety of craft beers and cocktails, and hosts live music and DJ events.

Salento - A Mediterranean-style bar that serves a variety of cocktails, wines, and tapas dishes.

Loftas - A multifunctional cultural center that hosts a variety of events, including concerts, art exhibitions, and dance parties.

Bix Baras - A cozy bar that offers a variety of beers and a laid-back atmosphere.

These are just a few of the many great bars and clubs in Vilnius. Be sure to also explore the city's many hidden speakeasies and cocktail bars, which offer a more intimate and exclusive atmosphere.

ACCOMMODATION

Finding the perfect accommodation is an essential part of any trip. Luckily, Vilnius has plenty of options to suit every budget and preference, from luxurious hotels to budget-friendly hostels. In this section, we will explore some of the best places to stay in the city and provide tips for finding the perfect accommodation for your needs.

Where to stay

When it comes to finding the perfect place to stay in Vilnius, there are many factors to consider, such as location, budget, and amenities. Here are some of the best areas to stay in the city:

Old Town - This is the most popular and touristy area of the city, and for good reason. Old Town is home to many of the city's top attractions, as well as a variety of restaurants, cafes, and bars. Accommodation options here range from luxurious hotels to budget-friendly hostels.

Užupis - This bohemian district is known for its artistic vibe and laid-back atmosphere. It's a great option for those looking to stay in a more unique and offbeat part of the city.

Žvėrynas - This quiet, residential neighborhood is a good choice for those who want to escape the hustle and bustle of the city center. It's located just a short distance from the city center and offers a variety of accommodation options, from hotels to apartments.

Naujamiestis - This neighborhood is becoming increasingly popular with young professionals and digital nomads. It's home to a variety of hip cafes, bars, and restaurants, as well as some great accommodation options.

When choosing where to stay in Vilnius, it's important to consider your priorities and preferences. If you're looking for a lively and central location, Old Town is the best option. If you prefer a more laid-back and bohemian atmosphere, Užupis is a good choice. No matter where you choose to stay, you're sure to fall in love with the charm and beauty of Vilnius.

Hotels, hostels, and guesthouses

Vilnius has a wide range of accommodation options to suit every budget and preference. Whether you're looking for a luxurious hotel, a budget-friendly hostel, or a cozy guesthouse, there's something for everyone in this beautiful city.

Hotels - Vilnius has many luxurious and high-end hotels, particularly in the Old Town area. These hotels offer a range of amenities, including restaurants, bars, spas, and fitness centers. Some of the most popular hotels in Vilnius include the Kempinski Hotel Cathedral Square, the Hotel PACAI, and the Narutis Hotel.

Hostels - If you're looking for budget-friendly accommodation, hostels are a great option. Vilnius has many hostels located throughout the city, offering shared dormitory rooms as well as private rooms. Some of the most popular hostels in Vilnius include Hostelgate, Jimmy Jumps House, and Fortuna Hostel.

Guesthouses - Guesthouses are a great option for those who want a more personalized and homey experience. Vilnius has many charming guesthouses located throughout the city, offering cozy rooms and friendly service. Some popular guesthouses in Vilnius include Bernardinu Guest House, Vilnius Home Bed and Breakfast, and B&B&B&B&B.

No matter what type of accommodation you're looking for, it's important to book in advance, particularly during peak season. Many hotels and hostels offer discounts for booking in advance, so be sure to shop around and compare prices to find the best deal.

Budget vs. luxury options

When it comes to accommodation in Vilnius, there are plenty of options to suit a range of budgets and preferences. Whether you're looking for a luxurious hotel or a budget-friendly hostel, you'll find plenty of choices.

Budget options - If you're traveling on a budget, there are plenty of affordable accommodation options in Vilnius. Hostels are a great option for budget-conscious travelers, with many offering shared dormitory rooms for as little as €10-€15 per night. There are also budget-friendly hotels and guesthouses throughout the city, with prices ranging from €30-€70 per night depending on location and amenities.

Luxury options - Vilnius also has a great selection of luxury accommodation options for those willing to splurge. Some of the most luxurious hotels in Vilnius can be found in the Old Town, offering stunning views and high-end amenities such as spas, fitness centers, and gourmet restaurants. Expect to pay upwards of €150 per night for a luxurious hotel experience.

Your choice of accommodation depends on your budget and travel style. A budget-friendly hotel or hostel is ideal for those on a tight budget, while a high-end hotel or guesthouse provides a more luxurious experience for those willing to splurge.

PRACTICAL INFORMATION

As with any travel destination, it's important to have some practical information about Vilnius before you go. From visa requirements to local customs and safety considerations, knowing the ins and outs of Vilnius can help ensure a smooth and enjoyable trip. In this section, we'll cover all the practical information you need to know before visiting Vilnius.

Money and tipping

The currency in Lithuania is the Euro. You can exchange your money at banks, exchange offices, and some hotels. Major credit cards are widely accepted, but it's a good idea to have some cash on hand for smaller purchases.

Tipping in Lithuania is not mandatory, but it's customary to leave a small amount for good service. In restaurants, it's common to leave a 10% tip if you're satisfied with the service. You can also tip taxi drivers and hairdressers, but it's not expected in other service industries.

Health and safety

Vilnius is generally a safe city, with low levels of violent crime. However, like any city, there are some safety considerations to keep in mind.

When it comes to health, it's always a good idea to have comprehensive travel insurance that covers medical expenses, including emergency repatriation. While there are good medical facilities in Vilnius, they can be expensive without insurance. It's also worth noting that some vaccines may be recommended before visiting Lithuania, such as Hepatitis A and B.

As for safety, pickpocketing and petty theft can occur, especially in crowded tourist areas. Keep your belongings close to you and be aware of your surroundings. It's also a good idea to take licensed taxis and avoid walking alone at night, especially in quiet or poorly lit areas. Finally, be cautious of scam artists who may try to take advantage of tourists, such as those who offer unsolicited tours or overly good deals.

Language and communication

In Lithuania, the predominant and official language is Lithuanian, which is spoken by a significant majority of the population. If you're visiting Vilnius or any other urbanized regions of the country, you'll find that many young Lithuanians are proficient in English and can converse with you fluently in this language. It's also worth noting that some of the locals might speak Polish or Russian, given the historical and cultural ties between Lithuania and these neighboring countries. However, you'll find that knowing some basic Lithuanian phrases can go a long way in bridging communication gaps and establishing a deeper connection with the people and culture of this beautiful Baltic nation.

In terms of written communication, most signs and menus in Vilnius are in Lithuanian, although many also have English translations. Some older locals may not speak English, but you can usually find someone nearby who can help translate if needed.

If you're planning on traveling to more rural areas outside of Vilnius, it's a good idea to learn a few basic phrases in Lithuanian to help you communicate with locals. Some useful phrases to know include "Labas" (hello), "Ačiū" (thank you), and "Atsiprašau" (excuse me). Overall, communication in Vilnius is generally not a problem, and you should be able to navigate the city with ease even if you don't speak Lithuanian.

Local customs and etiquette

When visiting Vilnius, it's important to be aware of local customs and etiquette to show respect for the culture and people of Lithuania. Here are some things to keep in mind:

Greetings: When meeting someone for the first time, it's customary to shake hands. In more casual situations, a nod or wave may suffice.

Dress code: While there is no strict dress code in Vilnius, it's generally a good idea to dress modestly and avoid revealing clothing, particularly when visiting religious sites.

Punctuality: Lithuanians are generally punctual and expect the same from others. It's considered rude to be late without giving notice.

Gift-giving: It's customary to bring a small gift, such as flowers or chocolates, when visiting someone's home. When giving a gift, it's polite to do so with both hands.

Tipping: Tipping is not mandatory in Lithuania, but it's common to leave a small amount for good service at restaurants, cafes, and bars. A tip of around 10% is usually sufficient.

Table manners: When dining in a formal setting, it's considered impolite to begin eating before the host or without being invited to do so. It's also important to keep your elbows off the table and avoid slouching.

By keeping these customs and etiquette in mind, you can show respect for the people and culture of Vilnius and have a more enjoyable and memorable trip.

Useful phrases and vocabulary

If you're planning a trip to Vilnius, it's a good idea to learn a few basic phrases and words in Lithuanian to help you communicate with the locals. Here are some useful phrases and vocabulary:

- Hello: Labas
- Goodbye: Viso gero
- Thank you: Ačiū
- Yes: Taip
- No: Ne
- Please: Prašau
- Excuse me: Atsiprašau
- I'm sorry: Atsiprašau
- Do you speak English?: Ar kalbate angliškai?
- How much is it?: Kiek tai kainuoja?
- Cheers!: Į sveikatą!
- Beer: Alus
- Wine: Vynas
- Food: Maistas
- Water: Vanduo

- Coffee: Kava
- Tea: Arbata

Learning a few basic phrases and words in Lithuanian can go a long way in making your trip more enjoyable and help you connect with the local culture.

DAY TRIPS FROM VILNIUS

Looking for an adventure outside of Vilnius? Look no further than the surrounding areas, where you can explore beautiful countryside, historic landmarks, and charming towns. Here are some of the top day trips from Vilnius that you won't want to miss.

Trakai(54°38'16.0"N 24°55'57.5"E)

Trakai is a historic town located just 28 kilometers west of Vilnius, known for its picturesque location on the shores of Lake Galvė and the stunning Trakai Island Castle. This former capital of the Grand Duchy of Lithuania is a popular day trip destination for visitors to Vilnius.

The Trakai Island Castle is the main attraction, a 14th-century fortress situated on an island in the middle of Lake Galvė. It is one of the most iconic landmarks in Lithuania and a must-visit for history enthusiasts. The castle has been restored to its former glory, with exhibitions on Lithuanian history, culture, and art.

Aside from the castle, Trakai is known for its scenic natural beauty, with forests, lakes, and rivers surrounding the town. Visitors can enjoy a variety of outdoor activities, such as hiking, cycling, and water sports.

Trakai is also famous for its traditional Karaim cuisine, a fusion of Turkish, Crimean Tatar, and Lithuanian flavors. Visitors can try Karaim specialties, such as kibinai, a pastry filled with meat or vegetables, or the famous cepelinai, a potato-based dish filled with meat or cheese.

To get to Trakai from Vilnius, you can take a train from Vilnius Railway Station or a bus from the Vilnius Bus Station. The journey takes approximately 30 minutes. Alternatively, you can hire a car and drive there yourself, which takes around 40 minutes.

Kernavė(54°53'12.1"N 24°51'17.1"E)

Located just a short drive from Vilnius, Kernavė is a small town that offers visitors a glimpse into Lithuania's rich history. The town is home to an impressive archaeological site that contains the remains of a medieval hill fort and several prehistoric settlements.

Visitors to Kernavė can explore the Archaeological Park, which features reconstructed ancient buildings, a museum, and a hiking trail that offers stunning views of the surrounding countryside. The park also hosts a number of cultural events throughout the year, including festivals celebrating Lithuanian music, dance, and food.

In addition to its archaeological attractions, Kernavė is also known for its beautiful natural surroundings. The town is located on the banks of the Neris River and is surrounded by rolling hills and forests, making it a popular destination for hiking, cycling, and fishing.

Kernavė is a great choice for visitors looking to experience Lithuania's rich cultural and natural heritage outside of the city.

Anykščiai(55°31'47.0"N 25°06'40.7"E)

Located about 110 km north of Vilnius, Anykščiai is a charming town that offers visitors an authentic Lithuanian experience. Surrounded by beautiful forests, hills, and rivers, the town is perfect for nature lovers and those who want to escape the hustle and bustle of the city.

One of the main attractions of Anykščiai is the treetop walking path, a 300-meter-long path that is 21 meters high and offers stunning views of the surrounding forests. Another must-see attraction is the Puntukas Stone, a giant boulder that is said to be the largest in Lithuania.

Visitors can also explore the narrow-gauge railway, which is the oldest surviving railway of its kind in Lithuania, and take a ride on a traditional horse-drawn carriage. The town is also home to a number of interesting museums, including the Ethnographic Museum and the Horse Museum.

For those who enjoy outdoor activities, Anykščiai offers opportunities for cycling, kayaking, and hiking. In the winter, visitors can also try their hand at skiing or snowboarding at the nearby ski resort.

Anykščiai is a great day trip destination for those who want to experience the natural beauty and cultural heritage of Lithuania.

Druskininkai(54°00'18.0"N 23°59'15.0"E)

Druskininkai is a spa town located in southern Lithuania, just a couple of hours away from Vilnius. This charming town is famous for its mineral springs and therapeutic mud, making it a popular destination for those looking for a relaxing and rejuvenating experience.

Druskininkai also has plenty of other attractions to

offer visitors. One of the most popular is the Grutas Park, also known as Stalin's World. This unique open-air museum displays sculptures and artifacts from the Soviet era, giving visitors a glimpse into Lithuania's recent history.

Another must-see attraction in Druskininkai is the Snow Arena, which is the only indoor ski slope in the Baltics. This 460-meter-long slope is perfect for skiing, snowboarding, and other winter sports, regardless of the weather outside.

For those interested in nature, Druskininkai is also home to the Dzukija National Park, which is the largest protected area in Lithuania. Here, visitors can explore the park's stunning landscapes, hike through forests, and observe wildlife such as wolves, lynx, and deer.

Druskininkai is a great destination for those looking for a mix of relaxation, culture, and adventure.

The Hill of Crosses(56°00'55.1"N 23°24'57.5"E)

A unique and spiritual pilgrimage site located about 2 hours north of Vilnius. Here you can see thousands of crosses and other religious symbols that have been placed on the hill over the years. The hill is covered in thousands of crosses, ranging in size from small handheld crosses to massive metal structures.

The crosses have been placed here over many decades by pilgrims seeking spiritual healing, protection, and blessings.

The origin of the Hill of Crosses is shrouded in mystery and legend. According to one story, the hill was created in the 1800s by Lithuanians who revolted against Russian rule and placed crosses on the hill as a symbol of their resistance. Another legend suggests that the hill was formed in the 1800s as a burial site for victims of an outbreak of cholera.

Over time, the Hill of Crosses has become an important pilgrimage site for Lithuanians and other Catholics. It has also been visited by many notable figures, including Pope John Paul II, who prayed at the hill during his visit to Lithuania in 1993.

Despite being destroyed by Soviet authorities multiple times during the 1900s, the Hill of Crosses has always been rebuilt by the faithful, and it continues to be a symbol of Lithuania's rich religious and cultural heritage.

Visiting the Hill of Crosses is an awe-inspiring experience, with its vast array of crosses representing a diverse range of styles and artistic expressions. Many visitors also leave their own crosses and other religious objects as a way of paying homage to this sacred site. For those seeking a deeper spiritual connection or a unique cultural experience, a visit to the Hill of Crosses is an unforgettable journey.

CONCLUSION

As your journey in Vilnius comes to an end, it's hard not to feel a sense of awe and appreciation for the beauty and rich history of this city. From its stunning architecture and landmarks to its vibrant arts scene and outdoor activities, Vilnius offers something for everyone. The local cuisine and hospitality will make you feel at home, and the day trips from Vilnius allow for further exploration of the Lithuanian countryside. Whether you're a history buff, a foodie, or an outdoor enthusiast, Vilnius is a destination that will leave a lasting impression. So pack your bags, grab your guidebook, and get ready for an unforgettable adventure in this magical city.

Final thoughts

Vilnius is a city that captures the hearts of all who

visit. Its rich history, stunning architecture, vibrant arts scene, and natural beauty are just a few of the reasons why it is such a popular destination. Whether you're interested in exploring the city's many landmarks and museums, immersing yourself in the local culture and cuisine, or simply enjoying the great outdoors, there is something for everyone in Vilnius.

With this guide, we hope to have provided you with a comprehensive overview of what Vilnius has to offer, from its fascinating history and culture to its top attractions, outdoor activities, food and drink, and practical information. We have also highlighted some of the best day trips you can take from the city, so you can get a taste of what the surrounding area has to offer.

We hope that this guide will inspire you to plan your own unforgettable trip to Vilnius. There is no shortage of things to see and do in this enchanting city, and we are sure that you will fall in love with it just as we have. Whether you are traveling solo, with friends, or with family, Vilnius is a destination that will leave a lasting impression and memories that will stay with you forever.

Milton Keynes UK
Ingram Content Group UK Ltd.
UKHW022038180823
427121UK00011B/1194

9 798393 333133